*From
the* RIVER
to the
RAT RACE

From the RIVER to the RAT RACE

A Former Riverboat Pilot Navigates Corporate America

PATRICK TRUE

Hillsboro Press
PROVIDENCE PUBLISHING CORPORATION
FRANKLIN, TENNESSEE

Copyright 2002 by Patrick True

All rights reserved. Written permission must be secured from the publisher to use or reproduce any part of this book, except for brief quotations in critical reviews or articles.

Printed in the United States of America

06   05   04   03   02   1   2   3   4   5

Library of Congress Catalog Card Number: 2001099066

ISBN: 1-57736-252-7

Cover design by Gary Bozeman

Cover photo by Patrick True

Illustrations by Lynn Thompson

238 Seaboard Lane Franklin, Tennessee 37067
www.providencepubcorp.com
800–321–5692

In memory of
DR. HUGH CLAUGHTON SR., D.V. M.

His love for animals was matched only by his love for boats.
As owner of the Belle Carol Riverboat Company,
he gave many kids their first opportunity to succeed.
I was fortunate to be one of those kids.

CONTENTS

PREFACE & ACKNOWLEDGMENTS	ix
CHAPTER 1 Go with the Flow	3
CHAPTER 2 Explore New Lessons around the Next Bend	12
CHAPTER 3 Enjoy the Company of Your Shipmates—It's Not That Big A Boat	20
CHAPTER 4 Control Your Own Wake—Your Actions Affect Others	27
CHAPTER 5 Come to the Aid of Others Who Need Assistance	33
CHAPTER 6 Take Time to Enjoy the Scenery	39
CHAPTER 7 Leave Port in Order to Make It to the Next Town	47
ABOUT THE AUTHOR	52

Preface & Acknowledgments

In May of 1978, at the age of fourteen, I embarked on an incredible journey that was to change my life forever. I stepped foot onto an authentic sternwheeler for the first time. I was reporting for duty as a bilge pumper and general roustabout for the Belle Carol Riverboat Company, operating on the Cumberland River. In boating terms, that meant that I was to assist the crew members and captains with all sorts of jobs, from pumping water out of the boat to repairing broken boards on the paddlewheel. This was truly the ground floor of the organization, the ultimate entry-level position.

The Belle Carol Riverboat Company had operated in Nashville since the late sixties and included two sternwheelers that were used to conduct daytime sightseeing cruises as well as evening dinner cruises. I had found my way onto the boats by virtue of my oldest sister, who had been hired to run the concessions during cruises.

I had been around water many times and had spent many a summer's day deep-sea fishing with my father and grandfathers in the Gulf of Mexico. This experience, however, was different. As I entered the vessel, I sensed that my journey had just begun and that many lessons awaited me.

Over the next eight years of my life, the river was to become my second home. I would transition from my role as bilge pumper to painter, oiler, deckhand, crew manager, and finally captain at the age of eighteen. It was more than just a summer job to fill the gaps between years of high school and college. It became the foundation for the rest of my life.

The pages of this book communicate some of the lessons I learned during this eight-year journey. Now that I have left the river and am in the fifteenth year of my professional business career, I can reflect on these lessons and realize how well they apply to life in everyday corporate America. The lessons that I will outline are quite simple in theory, but often difficult in practice—or at least I have found them to be.

1. Go with the flow
2. Explore new lessons around the next bend

Preface & Acknowledgments

3. Enjoy the company of your shipmates—it's not that big a boat
4. Control your own wake—your actions affect others
5. Come to the aid of others who need assistance
6. Take time to enjoy the scenery
7. Leave port in order to make it to the next town

Through these seven lessons, I will provide a unique perspective on what we so often refer to as the "rat race." By reading stories about life on the river, you can share in this journey and use it to advance your own position, both personally and professionally.

Special thanks to Dimples Kellogg for her editing expertise; Lynn Thompson for her wonderful illustrations; Andrew B. Miller and the staff of Providence Publishing Corporation for their skillful preparation of this book; and to the training team at Private Business, Inc. for motivating me to move forward with this project.

From the RIVER
to the RAT RACE

CHAPTER ONE

GO WITH THE FLOW

"The wind and the waves are always on the side of the ablest navigator."

—EDWARD GIBBON

What Edward Gibbon wrote more than two hundred years ago holds as true today as it did then. Any study of success will tell you that the steady performer, whether in business or any other walk of life, is one who can make the most of the external factors that impact his or her environment. On the river, I first experienced this by observing the seasoned captains. These men with thirty and forty years of experience were proven leaders in their field. I stood in awe as they displayed a consistent ability to bring the boats to safe harbor, no matter what the current, weather, and wind conditions. They even seemed to use

the conditions to their advantage. They worked with the environment rather than against it.

As a young pilot, I first tried to mimic their performance. I learned very quickly that it was much more difficult than it appeared. An eighty-foot vessel simply does not respond as well to a novice as it does at the hand of a master craftsman. As I gained more experience, my performance actually improved the more I relaxed and let the river flow beneath me. I realized that I couldn't control the current, wind, rain, or even the actions of other pilots. The more I let go, the better I became, and the more confidence I gained. This sounds simple, but it certainly isn't easy to let go. After all, isn't it human nature to want to control your environment?

By agreeing to go with the flow, you don't have to give up or give in. You don't have to compromise your beliefs and opinions. It is more a matter of using the environment to your advantage by establishing a keen awareness of your surroundings, keeping your eyes open, and anticipating changes. When piloting upstream against heavy currents, I learned when to stay out of the mainstream, when to cross it, and when to fight it. In much the same way, I learned how to use the conditions to gain momentum while piloting downstream.

Although I gained confidence with each new day, there were still times when it seemed that the challenge of piloting was greater than I could handle. On one occasion, I was piloting a sternwheeler on a dinner cruise when an unexpected storm hit. The cruise had started under clear summer skies, but the situation quickly grew dangerous. I was proceeding downstream about two miles from the dock when the boat was hit with fifty-mile-per-hour winds and heavy rain. Visibility was down to a few feet, and, to make matters worse, I knew that an interstate bridge stood less than half a mile away.

All I could do was to position a crew member on the bow and the stern to look for any obstacles and try to hold my position. Within fifteen minutes the storm cleared enough for me to make a run for the harbor. Five minutes after we landed we were hit again and had to cancel the remainder of the day.

The storm had not been predicted, and the severity of the situation had certainly awakened me to the fact that piloting boats could be as stressful as any other profession. For the first time in my piloting career, I was faced with the realization that I carried complete responsibility for all of my passengers and crew.

Every one of us shares a common challenge, no matter how we choose to make a living. We must deal with issues and with circumstances that are totally out of our control. We must somehow find a way to either work around or work through these circumstances to achieve our personal and professional goals. Sometimes we will be successful and sometimes we will fail. That's life, and it's just going to happen. The essence of success lies in continuing to pursue the dream during the bad times and the times when the spotlight is off.

Later in my career as a pilot, I savored the taste of success. There were days when my technique seemed flawless, and the boat went wherever I commanded. It was the river captain's equivalent to being in the "zone" that so many athletes describe after an outstanding performance. That taste of success was sweet, and it overpowered the other days when things didn't seem to flow as smoothly. When you are in the zone, though, you sense the ability to work within the confines of your environment. The zone is not about having everything go your way; it's about dealing successfully with the things that don't go your way. It's about a respect for the external factors that you must face on a daily basis.

After leaving the river, I realized that the same formula for success existed in the business sector, perhaps even to a greater degree because the pace of change was faster. After surviving my first three corporate mergers and a couple of downsizing initiatives, I realized that the current and the waves were just as dangerous on Main Street as they were on the waterways. The answers, however, were no different. It all still came down to my ability to anticipate change and to put myself in a position that would increase the likelihood of success.

The first skill I learned as a pilot was to anticipate the next bend and to position the boat as early as possible. Sternwheelers react very slowly and require even more diligence. I couldn't wait until the last minute and "make it up." I had to execute my plan early and adjust it often. Otherwise, I might be successful only some of the time.

To be a consistent performer you must work to perfect your technique. Even when you plan effectively and try to anticipate problems, the little surprises that life deals you may threaten your success. The ability to succeed despite those surprises is evidence of real greatness.

In the end, going with the flow is about attitude. It is about your ability to choose your state of mind everyday and to stick with it. If you can master your own attitude, your chances of success and happiness will dramatically improve whether you are on the river or on Main Street.

One particular event that took place on the boat represents a vivid example of a positive attitude. Our main daytime entertainer had decided to get married on one of the boats, and he had chartered it for a party of about one hundred people. The cruise took place during the spring rains when a lot of debris found its way off the riverbank and into the rising waters. In this case, the debris was a forty-foot submerged tree that lodged itself between our rudders. I was working the cruise as a deckhand and tried to free the massive log from the rudders, but to no avail. We were dead in the water and had to call for a towboat to take us in.

Such an occurrence could have ruined a wedding party, but it only seemed to add to the flavor of the moment. The people in attendance played off the attitude of the new bride and groom, and they had determined that nothing was going to spoil the day. The band played a few more songs, and the guests had a little extra cruising time. It was one of those situations that was totally out of everyone's control, and we just had to laugh about it.

Many times in life the unexpected will challenge you. The real challenge, though, is to maintain your momentum and to keep a positive attitude all the way through. You've got to go with the flow.

RIVER GUIDE
1. Think back to a time in your life where you felt that you were "in the zone."
   - How did you feel at that moment?
   - What was going right?
   - What external factors were you facing and how did you address them?
2. Think about a time at work when the "wind and the waves" seemed to be working against you.
   - How did you make it through?
   - What did you learn from the experience?
   - What changes did you make the next time you dealt with similar circumstances?

3. Can you recall a past situation where you had to deal with a totally unexpected event or circumstance?
    - How did you choose to react?
    - How did those around you react?

CHAPTER TWO

EXPLORE NEW LESSONS AROUND THE NEXT BEND

"True knowledge is to know the extent of one's own ignorance."

—CONFUCIUS

The concept of continuous improvement has worked its way into the fabric of American society since the dawn of the Industrial Revolution. In the past twenty years, we have begun to apply this concept to our own careers. To be competitive in a changing world, we must challenge ourselves to expand our knowledge almost daily.

On the river, this challenge was presented to me through a combination of tough love and encouragement. One captain took me under his wing during my first year and quietly encouraged me to learn. At first, his attention was a by-product of his fear that I was too young to accept the task at hand and that I would get hurt while performing the job. As he became more comfortable with me and with my desire to learn, the lessons became more complex. In one summer, this man taught a fourteen-year-old kid more about sternwheelers, rivers, mechanics, electronics, and plumbing than many people learn in a lifetime.

Of the lessons I learned, the most important was that I did not know everything and that I never would. That is tough for a fourteen-year-old to accept. Instead, the best that I could hope for was to improve my position every year through hard work and focus. This particular captain was one of two who were responsible for the advancement that I made every year on the boat.

Another captain also took me on as his student. His specialty was docking. When I met him, he had just retired as captain of a local ferry where he had landed boats for three decades. I will never forget the first time he allowed me to attempt a docking. I was sixteen, and I had spent a lot of time as a steersman, simply guiding the sternwheeler up and down the river. I had never been allowed to land it, though, which takes special skill. On this cruise, we had about two hundred passengers on board, and there were also a few hundred people waiting on the riverfront. After all, the riverboat was coming in, and this event has fascinated people since the invention of the paddlewheel. From small children to senior citizens, the sight of a sternwheeler rounding the bend always captures the imagination.

On this particular day, the captain decided that I was ready to give it a try. I will always remember his words as I prepared the boat for landing. Here I was, turning the boat upstream, walking it across the river by a combination of steering and engine handling. This procedure was a delicate balancing act between engine power, current, wind, and boat placement. If I were to approach the dock too quickly, I could cause damage to the boat and possible injury to passengers. The pressure began to set in as we made the turn and proceeded upstream toward the dock.

As we approached, I remember commenting about how many people were in attendance for the landing, quietly hoping that the captain would take the wheel out of my sweaty hands. Instead, he looked out the pilothouse window

and calmly observed the masses. He said, "Let me tell you the difference between a novice and an experienced pilot. As a man who has landed boats for thirty years, I look out at all of those nice folks on the dock, and I see spectators. As a young pilot trainee, I suppose that you look at the same people, and you see witnesses. You will know that you have made it when you enjoy the event as much as they do."

Over the years, I've thought a lot about those words. How many times have I decided not to do something because I never got past the "witness" stage? I have shared that story with many employees who were dealing with the challenges and stresses of a new job. After all, we are all novice trainees at some point in our lives. Just think about the first time that you used a computer or even a fax machine. Think about the first day in a new company on a new job. The room was filled with witnesses. Also remember the times when you were able to look upon them as spectators and peers.

You are living in an age when you must continue to learn new skills to even have a chance at advancement in corporate America. Consider the changes in your office environment over the last twenty years or even the last ten. Then consider that the pace of change is likely to double over the next ten years, if not five. You cannot stand still. Instead you must advance your knowledge in key areas that will support your expertise. At times you may even have to develop new areas of expertise. The point is that you are moving, growing, learning, and exploring.

My belief in the process of lifelong learning has now led me into a professional training career. It has become my passion. If not for my experiences on the boats, I would not have had the courage to change careers. While I have experienced both success and failure in my professional life, I have always tested my abilities and put myself into a position where I had to learn new skills. Public speaking is a good example. Like many people, I used to be terrified of the idea, much less the practice. Now I have given speeches for six years in front of large groups of people, and I actually enjoy the experience. It was never easy, and it took six months for the butterflies to go away. When I stand before a group now, however, I see spectators who used to be witnesses.

I once heard a great saying: "Courage is simply fear that has said its prayers." Don't be afraid to have a lot of witnesses in your future. Only then can you be assured of sharing some wonderful experiences with the spectators of your life.

True commitment to lifelong learning involves a level of discipline that is hard to maintain. During our lifetimes, most of us will see that intensity fade and then strengthen many times. Often success will trigger a desire to pursue a greater dream. At times, failure will serve as the catalyst for change. When you find your momentum slipping, consider this story from an anonymous author:

> Man O'War was the greatest racehorse who ever lived. In his lifetime he ran only twenty-one races. His total racing time was thirty-three minutes and thirty-two seconds. Stop and think about that. Think about it—in all his life Man O'War ran in competition for only half an hour. His fame as the greatest racehorse of all time was built on just that half hour. That's what history remembers—only his races in competition.
>
> But the days and the weeks and the months of stubborn and relentless training—the days and the weeks and the months with no one in the

grandstands—with no one to cheer him on but his own pride and ambition—these were the important things. These were the things that really made him a champion. You see, he was good when he didn't have to be. He was good when no one else was watching. And that, my friends, is the true mark of a thoroughbred.

You are the only one who can motivate yourself to succeed in the practice of lifelong learning. The victories may help carry you to the next race, but the true test will be how you perform during the journey itself.

RIVER GUIDE
1. Think back to a time in your life when you started to see spectators where witnesses used to stand. What were the circumstances?
2. What professional or personal dream are you currently pursuing?
3. What will it take to achieve your goals?
4. Where are you in the process?
5. What is your next step?

CHAPTER THREE

Enjoy the Company of Your Shipmates — It's Not That Big a Boat

"The greater part of our happiness or misery depends on our disposition and not on our circumstances."

—Martha Washington

One key memory that I will always take away from my life on the river is the people. Not just the captains I have mentioned, but the countless crew members, caterers, actors, entertainers, mechanics, and guests. For eight years, these people served as the cast members in what was to me a wonderful, almost surreal, existence apart from everything that I was experiencing at the time in school. The boats really were my second home for this period. During the summers, I would spend every waking hour on them, and in the winters I would help to maintain them for the off-season.

Enjoy the Company of Your Shipmates 21

    While this diverse group of people did not have much in common outside of our work, we served as an extended family to each other on the boats. Some were college students, some were retired captains. Some were drifters, and one claimed to be a rodeo rider. And all shared two characteristics. First, there was always an intense sense of camaraderie and teamwork. Second, there was a shared understanding that, through it all, we were there to have fun.

    In my third year on the boats, I witnessed what to this day is the best example of teamwork in which I have ever been privileged to participate. The owner of the company decided that we would attempt to run not one but two dinner cruises in a single evening. As far as I know, we were the first touring company in the country to attempt this. It required the employees of the boat as well as the caterers to work in absolute harmony during an intense thirty-minute period.

    Between 8:00 P.M., when the boat landed, and 8:30 P.M., when it was to depart, we had to safely allow one hundred and fifty passengers to leave the vessel, clean both decks, service both engines, reload the buffet line, and load another hundred or so passengers onto the boat. Through it all, everyone needed to maintain a strong sense of customer service and have fun with the passengers. The pace of the work was so fast that afterward, when the new cruise was under way, I would often climb up to the pilothouse and collapse both mentally and physically. In the end, though, we became so good at this task that we eventually added a midnight dance cruise to the roster.

Even though the work was intense, we found many occasions to cut up and joke with each other, often including the passengers. On one such occasion, I was taking a break from the pilothouse during a daytime cruise. The entertainer on the first deck was playing to a crowd of about eighty senior citizens. I was leaning against the bar and talking to the bartender when I unwittingly became the center of a practical joke. The entertainer standing near the bow of the boat began explaining to the crowd that their pilot for the cruise also happened to be an accomplished singer. This captain had even been invited to play on the Grand Ole Opry from time to time. He then spotlighted me and invited me to come forward to accompany him in song.

Now, absolutely none of this was true, but none of the passengers realized it. They were on their feet clapping and encouraging me to take up the offer. I was stuck, with no hope of escape. Inside I realized that this was payback for a joke I had played on the entertainer the week before. I had no choice but to play along. By the time I got to the stage, he had announced that we would sing "You Are My Sunshine" in the key of C. I pulled out about twenty keys on a chain I had in my pocket and asked him which one that was. The crowd laughed, then we started the song. Actually, I was in good shape into the second verse when I heard a guy in the first row turn to his wife and say, "Hey, he's pretty good!" That's when I became overconfident. By the end of the song, I had hit every note on the chart and just wanted to crawl back to the pilothouse. It just goes to show that paybacks can be rough.

These two stories are just remnants of literally hundreds like them over the years. As I left the boat, these experiences helped me immensely. First, I never took myself too seriously again, at least at work. Second, I entered into a business career with the complete

Enjoy the Company of Your Shipmates 25

understanding that in the end, it is all about the people.

Today, many of us spend the majority of our waking hours in the service of our employers. We spend all of this time with our coworkers, our second family away from home. We had better enjoy their company, or it's going to be a long day, a long week, and a long career.

I chose one of my favorite quotes by Martha Washington to open this chapter because I feel that it conveys a message for all of us in relating to our coworkers. From day to day we are likely to be confronted with issues that cause stress in the workplace. Many will involve conflict between individual employees. We would be living in a dreamworld if we thought otherwise.

In such times, we have to allow our disposition to pull us through and to conquer our circumstances. It really is not that big a boat that we all live in. The people you are sitting across from today at the office could be the same people that put in a good word to help you land your next job. You won't always agree with them, but your success may be determined by how you choose to act when you disagree—and how you get through it.

Take every chance you get to build closer professional relationships. Team assignments and projects may be more difficult than solitary work, but they can often offer a greater reward. Do not fear conflict. Recognize that everyone will have an opinion and disagreements are bound to occur. Most of all use these experiences to have some fun. If you are going to spend the majority of your waking hours on the job, you should enjoy it.

RIVER GUIDE
1. What is your favorite personal example of professional teamwork?
2. How important are your coworkers to your current office environment?
3. In what ways do you gain confidence from your inclusion in the team?
4. How do the members of your team deal with conflict?

Chapter Four

Control Your Own Wake — Your Actions Affect Others

"He who throws dirt loses ground."

—*Anonymous*

One of the most important rules of the road for pilots involves the "no wake" zone. This rule applies to any boat entering or exiting a harbor, and it exists for the purpose of reducing damage to boats and injury to their passengers as they sit defenseless in the close confines of an enclosed space.

Despite widespread knowledge of the rule, it seemed as though once a week a large houseboat would fly through the harbor with reckless abandon, oblivious to the chaos that was being inflicted upon other boats in the area. The captains of these vessels were either untrained or uncaring, and only rarely would they be punished for their deeds.

I didn't know the pilots of these boats, but I formed an initial opinion about them based solely on their actions. Those actions were even that much more disturbing to us while we were involved in complex operations such as the loading or unloading of passengers. In fact, we would have to suspend any operations until all of the waves cleared. Often, this delay resulted in the cruise departing late from the harbor, not to mention causing several dents in the boat.

Two general rules of physics also applied to the "no wake" requirement. The first involved the size of the vessel. The larger the boat, the more critical it was to comply with the rule. Second, the more crowded the harbor, the more important it was to comply. A large boat in a crowded harbor could do untold amounts of damage to smaller craft.

Now that I look back on more than fifteen years in business, I can clearly see that the "no wake" rule is also violated day after day in corporations across our country. Think of all the times a manager moved into an ongoing project with reckless abandon, oblivious to the chaos that he or she was causing within other departments.

Control Your Own Wake

Today we work in a world of complex systems and operations, where several groups may be attempting to coordinate activities in close proximity to one another. It is more important than ever to mind the speed of your craft and to consider the ramifications of your own actions. The same rules of physics apply. The more power you have and the more people around you, the more careful you must be in controlling your wake.

Toward the end of my career on the river, I can recall an example of a manager entering the company and violating the "no wake" zone. We had expanded the company with the addition of a new state-of-the-art craft that seated twice as many as our other boats. With it came a new crew manager, who had responsibility over all crewmembers. The company even began hiring its own food service staff, along with general crewmembers, hostesses, and bartenders.

Although this manager had no experience operating boats, he was also managing the nautical deckhands, who were responsible for the safety of the passengers and the mechanical operation of the boat. Many of the crewmembers resisted his authority, especially as he called for a new working schedule,

more formal uniforms, and a more regimented atmosphere. Both customer service and employee retention deteriorated as the result of his actions.

The crew would have readily accepted many of the initiatives of the new manager if he had obeyed the "no wake" rule. If he had simply observed the sense of team spirit that we all had developed through years of working together, he could have used that to his advantage. He should have moved in more slowly and observed the operations already in progress.

Since witnessing his actions, I have always promised myself that I would never make the same mistake. I will never enter a new position or an ongoing project with the intent of making immediate adjustments just for the sake of change. Instead, my preference is to observe, to see what is working and what is not. Later, armed with that information, I can begin to modify the processes as needed.

The way that we treat others speaks volumes for the quality of the organization. An atmosphere of respect will foster strong working relationships and even friendships. It will also be obvious to those outside looking in as potential clients or employees.

In addition to operations, the "no wake" rule should apply to communication within the office. Sometimes a person's "wake" is represented by comments made about other teams or other employees. In some cases, these comments can be just as damaging as the waves were to our boats—and longer lasting. We should all take note of the fact that our actions can cause a ripple effect through the organization. Whether it involves sexual harassment, racial discrimination, or other mistreatment of a fellow employee, our words and actions can be felt long after we have left the scene. As mentioned at the beginning of this chapter, we lose ground every time this happens. Such actions tend to erode the fabric of the team, just as a heavy wake erodes the shoreline of the harbor.

River Guide
1. Can you think of cases where you witnessed someone violating the "no wake" rule in the office? What happened?
2. How did others close to the situation feel?
3. What was the outcome?
4. Can you think of a time when you or someone close to you became the victim of a "no wake" violation through a personal comment made by a coworker?

CHAPTER FIVE

COME TO THE AID OF OTHERS WHO NEED ASSISTANCE

"You must never think of anything but the need, and how to meet it."

—CLARA BARTON

On a cool night in the fall of 1983, I was standing watch in the pilothouse during a dinner cruise. Despite the cool weather, I had the windows open and was enjoying the first real change in temperatures after a long, hot summer. Little did I know it, but having that window open may very well have saved somebody's life before the evening was over.

As the sternwheeler passed a local boat ramp, I heard a faint sound coming from the tree-lined riverbank. I lit up the spotlight and searched the bank. Sure enough, I spotted a man waving his arms and then pointing out into the river. As I searched his line of direction, I saw the nose of a boat pointing straight up and out of

Come to the Aid of Others Who Need Assistance 35

the water about sixty feet off my starboard bow. After searching further, I located a man in the water floating near his sinking craft.

Once I identified the location of the victim, I sounded the horn with five quick blasts, an action that brought another pilot to the pilothouse. I then gave the wheel to him and headed down to the bow to attempt a rescue operation. We turned the sternwheeler to face upstream, but it was still a difficult extraction since the sinking craft was in the vicinity and our boat sat more than four feet off the water.

The man in the water was so cold that he couldn't make an attempt to grasp the life ring that I was tossing in his direction. After what seemed like an eternity, I was able to get a line on him and, with the help of a few passengers, pull him up into the boat. In the process, we had phoned ahead for emergency personnel to meet us at the dock. Fifteen minutes after the extraction, we arrived and placed him in the ambulance.

There was nothing spectacular about this particular operation. I had seen it repeated by other pilots and crewmembers at least five times during my adventures on the river. It is the golden rule of any waterway that if you are the first to come to the scene of an accident, you are the one responsible for taking action. On the water you never know when, or if, anyone else will come by in time to offer assistance.

I personally believe this causes the sense of unity felt by so many men and women who spend a lot of time on the water, whether it be a river, lake, or the open ocean. No matter what the predicament, everyone is willing to get involved and lend a helping hand. This is a responsibility that comes from a deep respect for the water and the danger it can represent.

For the most part, I have also found that people are willing to lend a helping hand away from the water. Almost every day on the evening news, you can see some examples. Whether it is a daring rescue attempt or someone helping out at a local blood drive, it is nice to witness one person coming to the aid of another.

A few years ago, I was the one to be rescued. My wife had been ill for several weeks. For reasons unknown, her right lung had collapsed three times in the space of a month, and the doctors were exploring their options. She had spent the better part of thirty days in the hospital, and I was trying to juggle my time with her with my responsibility for our two toddlers as well as projects at work. As I look back, this time certainly falls in the top three or four most stressful points in my life.

During one critical moment of the ordeal, I found myself alone in her hospital room. Overnight, her lung had collapsed for the third time, and we had rushed to the emergency room. It was the next morning, and surgery was under way. We were both simply worn out and emotionally drained. There in that hospital room, I was looking for a lifeline, something to hold onto. Other than a quick voice mail to my boss the night before, no one but family knew the latest on the situation. It was at that moment that my boss and the president of the company walked into the hospital room.

They told me that everything was covered at work, and that I shouldn't worry. They told me to concentrate on my wife and kids. They assured me that their prayers and those of my coworkers were with me. Their visit was quick but powerful, and it gave me strength. No matter where I go professionally, I will always remember their effort. They gave me a lifeline of support at a desperate time that was every bit as strong as the lifeline I had thrown to the man fifteen years earlier.

No matter where you go in life, no matter what level of status or wealth you achieve, be willing to assist others in need. As our society grows more crowded and people are hit with strong messages of violence and disaster almost daily, there may be a tendency to become desensitized to the need. There may be a temptation to assume that someone else will come along to help. Please don't give in to this temptation. Whether you are helping during a crisis or offering a hand at the office, get involved, and make it happen. Even a simple act of kindness can mean everything to someone who is at the other end of the line.

River Guide
1. Think about a time when you were the rescuer, even if it was a simple act of kindness.
2. How did it make you feel?
3. What about the person you rescued?
4. Now think about a time when you were on the other end of the lifeline. What was the situation and how did you respond?

CHAPTER SIX

TAKE TIME TO ENJOY THE SCENERY

"Dost thou love life, then do not squander time, for that's the stuff life is made of."

—BENJAMIN FRANKLIN

I will never forget the feeling of inner peace that can be experienced simply by watching a river flow by. One of the greatest joys that a river pilot can experience is to stand watch on a calm, moonlit night. I can remember feeling a warm summer breeze meandering through the pilothouse. Toward the stern, I could hear the soft "whoosh, whoosh, whoosh" as the paddlewheel gently grabbed the water at half speed. Out the front pilothouse window, I could see the moon shining down onto the upper deck and the Tennessee flag gently flowing in the breeze. It was a special time, and it certainly contrasted with the hustle and bustle of the long, hot summer days. Even today, when I'm feeling stressed, I often recall those memories to calm my nerves.

During the summer of 1986, I was working as a first mate on a new luxury sternwheeler in Nashville. This vessel featured a six-hundred-seat theater and a full complement of actors, including a man whose job was to portray Mark Twain. I had seen this actor out of costume, but I'd never really talked to him. I had always heard that as soon as he was in full make-up, he would not leave character.

On one moonlit evening, I was enjoying a break from the pilothouse and was leaning against the rail on the hurricane deck. The outer decks of the boat were empty since everyone was attending the show inside. I can remember looking through a light fog toward the bow of the boat and seeing a man with white hair and a white suit approach.

The next few minutes were like a dream as I began a conversation with this actor, who was still portraying Twain. He talked about the river and his experiences as a young pilot. He asked me about my river experiences. I cannot quite describe what this conversation felt like, but it was the closest thing to time travel that I

have ever experienced. This conversation with Twain took place just a few months before the end of my river journey, and I will always look back on it as one of the most special conversations I ever had on the boats.

Moments like the ones I have described add a quality to our lives that cannot be replaced. I would imagine that most people could recall experiences that have a similar calming affect. Maybe it is a moment spent with a child or a spouse. Maybe it involves a certain peaceful place or time. Whatever it is, it serves as a kind of home base in your mind during times of stress or conflict. It helps to bring you back to center.

As we proceed down our chosen paths, we all have this in common. We are all challenged to make the most of our time here. Time is, in fact, the very essence of life and cannot be replaced. Our lives are not about a beginning and an end. They aren't about some final destination. They are about the journey itself. This sounds like the simplest of all the lessons in the book. Yet, it is the hardest to implement.

It seems that we get caught up in day-to-day events. For many of us the day is simply represented as a series of tasks and duties. They extend themselves into weeks and months. Before we realize it, another year has gone by. Our lives become something that is happening to us rather than something we have the opportunity to direct.

Every once in a while we are jolted out of this mundane existence by a critical turning point in our lives such as the birth of a child or the death of a loved one. It makes us stop and reflect on our real purpose. It may even make us adjust and savor our experiences more fully. Before long, however, most of us tend to get pulled back into the routine of life. We wake up, go to work, come home, have dinner, watch television, and go to sleep.

I have found only two ways to break this cycle. The first involves life at work and the second involves friends, family, and spirituality.

The first step in destroying the cycle and enjoying your time more fully is to move yourself into a direction that will allow you to pursue your professional dreams. Find your passion and set a plan in place that will allow you to live it. Let go of your fears and take steps toward your goal. Maybe you have found a career that is fulfilling, and it continues to enrich your life daily. Or maybe you are still searching. Granted, you have to be realistic. You have to live within your means and your capabilities, but you can still pursue your dreams.

I have a friend at work who keeps a personal journal. He happens to be one of the most successful people in our organization. His journal is different from any other I have seen because it is a "future" journal. It outlines his goals for the months and years to come. If he wants to achieve something in five years, he will put that in his journal. He will then break that goal into smaller goals until he eventually knows what he needs to do over the course of the next week or even the next day to achieve that goal. His goals energize him because he believes in them. They allow him to live his passion every day.

For me, the pursuit of a pilot's license represented the first major goal in my life. To be licensed by the Coast Guard, an applicant had to have four years of study on the waterway he would pilot and had to be at least eighteen years of age. The Coast Guard exams were challenging, and the study was intense. After working so hard for four years, I found it extremely satisfying to fulfill this goal and to begin piloting. More important, the success in reaching that goal motivated me to pursue other goals in my life, such as a college degree.

Take Time to Enjoy the Scenery 45

No matter how much I enjoy whatever challenges my work life brings, it will never match the joy that I gain daily from relationships with family and friends. Even still, when I get caught up in the cycle of day-to-day living, I often realize that my relationships have suffered through simple neglect. In fact, they are usually the first things to go. The only way to prevent this from happening is to recognize that it takes daily effort to keep my relationships alive. I've got to spend time nurturing them. I've got to invest the effort. It involves sacrifice, but the reward will be outstanding.

In addition to our professional lives and our relationships, many of us choose to spend time nurturing our spiritual identity. Over the years, my beliefs have served as an anchor and helped me to find a balance in my life. Ever since my days on the boats, I have carried a prayer with me, and I usually read it at least once a week. For me, it puts everything into perspective:

> My Lord God, I have no idea where I am going. I do not know the road ahead of me. I cannot know for certain where it will end. Nor do I really know myself, and the fact that I think I am following your will does not mean that I am actually doing

so. But I believe that the desire to please you does in fact please you. And I hope that I have that desire in all that I am doing. I hope that I will never do anything apart from that desire. And I know that if I do this you will lead me by the right road, though I may know nothing about it. Therefore I will trust you always though I may seem to be lost, and in the shadow of death. I will not fear, for you are ever with me, and you will never leave me to face my perils alone.

Thomas Merton

We must all make the choice daily to nourish our careers, our relationships, and our beliefs. Our efforts will typically be rewarded by special moments that enlighten our time here. These moments become our most cherished memories. In fact, they define who we are as people.

RIVER GUIDE
1. Think back to a time or place that holds special memories. How do these memories make you feel?
2. How would you define your true passions in life?
3. In what ways are you living your dream?
4. If you aren't, what do you plan to do about it?

CHAPTER SEVEN

LEAVE PORT IN ORDER TO MAKE IT TO THE NEXT TOWN

"Far better to dare mighty things, to win glorious triumphs, even though checkered by failure, than to rank with those poor spirits who neither enjoy much nor suffer much, because they live in the gray twilight that knows not victory, nor defeat."

— THEODORE ROOSEVELT

We had a simple saying on the boats. Whenever threatened by procrastination, we would say, "Don't put it off; put it on." When something needed to be repaired or built, there were usually at least four capable hands for the job. There was a real "can-do" attitude. The owners of the boat were also very willing to launch new initiatives without fear of failure. I can safely say that this atmosphere within the company came from them, from the top down. It was also contagious as many employees began to realize that they had a lot to offer.

During my senior year of college and my eighth year on the boats, I, too, was faced with the challenge to launch a new initiative. At that point, I felt the need to leave the nest that had been created for me on the boats. To make a career in boating, I would want to pursue a more advanced license that would allow me to pilot larger vessels.

As luck would have it, a huge new boat had just been built and introduced into the Nashville market. I can remember all the fanfare that surrounded this three-hundred-foot sternwheeler as it made its maiden voyage into Nashville. When it passed through the harbor, I can remember thinking that no matter what, I was going to find a way to land a job on it.

My first step was to interview with a local company that had been contracted to navigate the vessel for the first two years it was in town. After a few meetings, I had secured a position as one of two first mates on the boat. The job would also allow me to act as steersman and to study for a license that would allow me to pilot boats of any size. It was a huge thrill to be part of such a new and exciting venture. I had taken the next step and was ready to proceed.

Six months into the experience, I had found new friends and had enjoyed myself immensely. I had also discovered, however, that I was ready to leave the river behind.

After eight years, I knew that my life was taking a different turn. I wanted to settle down. I didn't want to move on to the larger excursion vessels that often required a pilot to be away from home for months at a time.

Most of us find that our lives will reach intersections from time to time, where we need to make a choice. It might involve a spouse or a job or a transfer to a new city. It might involve the challenge to return to school to earn an advanced degree. Whatever the choice, it is important to make it and to move on.

Too often our fears enter the picture, and we become locked in indecision. Many of us are just not cut out to be risk takers, and that's fine. Nevertheless, we need to take a stand and move toward our goals. Life is all about choices. We are bound to make mistakes, but we are also bound to succeed from time to time.

When I stepped foot off the boats for the last time, I was both proud and scared. I was proud of the eight-year achievement. It was hard to believe that I had gone from a fourteen-year-old kid to a twenty-two-year-old experienced pilot. It didn't seem real. I had worked harder than I ever imagined, sometimes clocking more than eighty hours a week. At the same time, I was

Leave Port in Order to Make It to the Next Town

scared to be leaving the familiar atmosphere of the river.

As I began a career in banking, there were new challenges and new initiatives. Soon I would decide to pursue a master's degree, and that would begin a whole new journey. Through it all, however, I never forgot the times on the river and the lessons I had learned. In the end, I found that I had learned a lot more about life than about boating. Though I was still far from knowing it all, I knew enough to count my blessings and to be thankful for having the chance to take the journey.

> Twenty years from now you will be more disappointed by the things that you didn't do than by the ones that you did. So throw off the bowlines. Sail away from safe harbor. Catch the trade winds in your sails. Explore. Dream. Discover.
>
> Mark Twain

Wherever your life takes you, I hope that some of the lessons reviewed in this book will make a difference. You are on a journey like no other. It is yours and yours alone to experience. Make the most of it. Live life to its fullest, and be sure to enjoy the cruise.

About the Author

Patrick True grew up in Nashville, Tennessee, where, at the age of fourteen, he worked for eight years as a crew member and later a pilot of authentic sternwheelers operating on the Cumberland River. After leaving the river, he began a career in commercial banking and later moved into the field of corporate training. Today, he serves as director of training for Private Business, Inc. in Brentwood, Tennessee. He holds a bachelor's degree in business administration from Belmont University and a master's in business administration from Middle Tennessee State University.

Patrick lives with his wife and children in Brentwood, Tennessee.